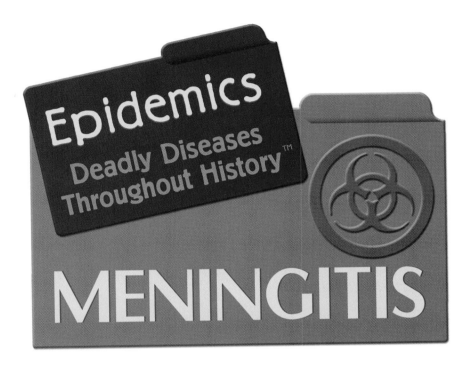

MARTHA KNEIB

Epidemics
Deadly Diseases
Throughout History™

MENINGITIS

The Rosen Publishing Group, Inc.
New York

*To Tom and Bobbi Kneib*

Published in 2005 by The Rosen Publishing Group, Inc.
29 East 21st Street, New York, NY 10010

**Library of Congress Cataloging-in-Publication Data**

Kneib, Martha.
Meningitis/by Martha Kneib.—1st ed.
p. cm.—(Epidemics)
Includes bibliographical references and index.
ISBN 1-4042-0257-9 (library binding)
1. Meningitis—Juvenile literature. 2. Meningitis—History—
Juvenile literature.
I. Title. II. Series.
RC376.K64 2005
616.8′2—dc22

                                        2004016701

*Manufactured in the United States of America*

**On the cover:** An image of tissue infected with meningitis after exposure to the anthrax bacterium.

# CONTENTS

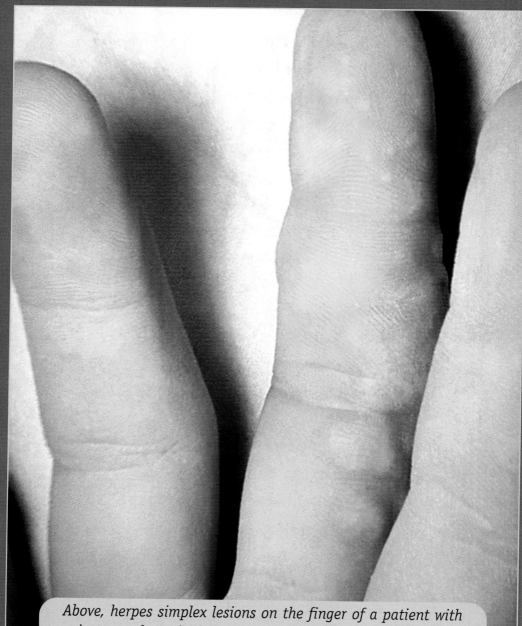

*Above, herpes simplex lesions on the finger of a patient with meningococcal meningitis. Herpes simplex II can cause recurrent forms of meningitis such as Mollaret's meningitis.*

# INTRODUCTION

Imagine that you are home one day when suddenly you don't feel well. After a few hours, you start to have the chills and your forehead feels hot. You have a fever. Soon you feel very tired. You will probably take some medicine like aspirin and go to bed, thinking you have the flu.

Soon, though, other symptoms arise. A rash appears on your body. Your neck becomes stiff, and you have a terrible headache, worse than ever before. Now you suspect this is something more serious than a case of the flu. Other symptoms that might develop can include nausea, discomfort in bright light, and confusion.

When anyone develops symptoms like this, it's time to visit the emergency room. If you don't get help quickly once symptoms like stiff neck and confusion set in, you stand the chance of suffering seizures, coma, or even death.

As soon as you come to the hospital with these symptoms, the doctors and nurses pay attention. They will be very concerned that your headache, stiff neck, and rash signify a potentially deadly disease. Before they even learn you have meningitis, they will administer strong antibiotics, just in case. They may also give you a steroid to reduce cranial swelling.

In order to determine if you have meningitis, they will remove fluid from around your spinal cord for testing. This fluid should be clear. If it is cloudy, you have a very serious infection. For a positive identification of what is making you ill, the lab technician will grow the bacteria in your spinal fluid in a culture in the lab. Within a few hours, the doctor will give you the diagnosis: you have meningitis.

# 1

# TYPES OF MENINGITIS

Meningitis is an infection of the meninges. The meninges are the three layers of membranes surrounding the brain and spinal cord. The outermost layer of the meninges is the dura mater, the central layer is the arachnoid, and the layer closest to the brain is the pia mater. In between these layers is a liquid called cerebrospinal fluid that protects the brain.

Infections reach the meninges by entering the cerebrospinal fluid. At this point, the meninges become irritated and swollen. This swelling is what produces the classic meningitis symptoms of stiff neck and headache. Bacterial meningitis is common in the United States; at least 25,000 cases are diagnosed each year.

Meningitis is sometimes difficult to detect in infants and small children because its classic symptoms may be subtle or absent. A baby cannot tell you that he or she has a headache, so doctors must be very observant in order to properly diagnose what is wrong. A baby with meningitis may display irritability, lack of appetite, and/or vomiting. At any age, seizures may result as the disease progresses, followed by coma and death.

Meningitis can originate from many different causes, including viral, fungal, bacterial, parasitic, cancerous, and chemical.

# Viral Meningitis

One of the most common, but least dangerous, forms of meningitis is viral meningitis. Viral meningitis will normally clear up by itself without complications. Viral meningitis is sometimes called aseptic meningitis when doctors attempt but fail to produce a positive identification of the underlying virus. Nearly every aseptic meningitis is caused by a virus.

Many different viruses can cause meningitis, including herpes simplex types 1 and 2, mumps, influenza, Epstein-Barr, measles, rubella, and polio, among others. The most common causes of viral meningitis are enteroviruses. These viruses normally live in the intestines. Enteroviruses like coxsackie and echovirus are often the cause of viral meningitis. Since many people who have it do not get sick enough to seek medical attention, it is difficult to know how wide-spread viral meningitis might be. Statistics are only available for the cases severe enough to require hospitalization.

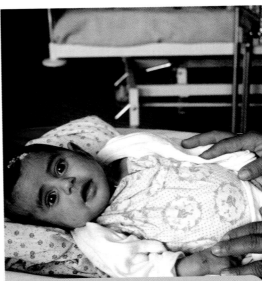

*A child sick with viral meningitis contracted from polluted water is treated in Iraq in 2004. The war in Iraq made fresh water and health care harder to find for many poor Iraqis.*

In populations where vaccinations are common, some of these causes of meningitis are rare. In the United States, for instance, meningitis from the mumps would be extremely unusual. However, in unimmunized populations, a full 30 percent of the people who contract the mumps virus will develop viral meningitis. Strangely, males are two to five times more likely than females to develop viral meningitis in this way.

Occasionally, the rates of aseptic meningitis rise. During the months of January through August of

1991, for example, 636 cases of aseptic meningitis were reported to the New York State Department of Health. This represented a 153 percent increase over the average number of cases for this period. The viruses responsible for this outbreak were coxsackie and echoviruses.

Other viruses that may cause meningitis include those spread by mosquitoes and ticks, like the St. Louis encephalitis virus, the eastern equine encephalitis virus, and the Colorado tick fever virus.

# Fungal Meningitis

Fungi can also cause meningitis. *Candida, Histoplasma, Coccidioides*, and *Cryptococcus* fungi have all been responsible for meningitis infections. Most cases of fungal meningitis occur in people who are already sick with a disease like AIDS, which has suppressed their immune systems. The fungi that cause meningitis are found in the environment and are spread on air currents. Healthy people will not develop meningitis from breathing in these particles. Several of these fungi are found in soil, and others, like *Candida*, are found everywhere, including on human skin and inside the intestines.

Meningitis caused by *Coccidioides immitis* is called coccidioidal meningitis. If left untreated, it is usually fatal. This fungus lives in the soil, and people develop this infection by inhaling fungal particles into their lungs. *C. immitis* can be found in the southwestern United States, Mexico, and Central and South America.

# Parasitic Meningitis

Larval worms traveling throughout the human body can also cause meningitis. One worm that sometimes causes the disease is *Strongyloides stercoralis*. This worm lives in tropical and subtropical areas. The adult worms live in the intestines, and their eggs are expelled from the body in the feces.

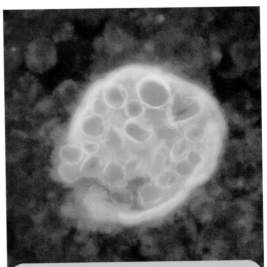

Pictured above is a microscopic image of endospores of the Coccidioides immitis *fungus. This fungus usually causes a lung disease known as coccidioidomycosis, which can then lead to meningitis.*

Once the eggs hatch, the new worms can enter a person through their skin. From there, they migrate to the lungs, travel to the throat, are swallowed, and develop into adults inside the intestines. The worms can survive in the soil for several generations without being parasites before they find a host.

Sometimes, these worms travel to other parts of the body like the liver or the meninges. If they reach the meninges, the infected person will develop meningitis.

Exposure to soil that is contaminated with human feces is the main way to catch this parasite, which is more prevalent in tropical environments. The only way to keep people from being infected is to eliminate exposure to contaminated soil.

Another worm that can cause problems is the rat lungworm, which is common only in Southeast Asia and the Pacific islands. However, it has also been found in Puerto Rico, Africa, and Louisiana, and was probably brought to these places by infected rats arriving from foreign ports. The eggs leave the rat in feces and develop in an intermediate host like a snail, crab, or shrimp. Humans can get the worm from eating undercooked seafood. From the intestines, these worms can travel throughout the body, including to the meninges. Other worms that can infect such animals as dogs, cats, and raccoons are spread in the same way. People can acquire these worms by eating undercooked food. The main way to avoid infection by parasites is to cook all food thoroughly, heating it to a high enough temperature to kill parasites.

Amoebas, which are single-celled organisms, can also cause parasitic meningitis. One of the species of amoebas that attacks humans is *Naegleria fowleri.* These amoebas have been found in lakes, swimming pools, ponds, rivers, tap water, and soil. The amoebas invade the body through the nasal passages. This form of meningitis is called primary amebic meningoencephalitis. In its most serious form, primary amebic meningoencephalitis can kill a healthy person within seventy-two hours. To avoid this form of meningitis, people should not swim in fresh lakes, ponds, and rivers. Ensuring that swimming pools are properly chlorinated and that tap water has been treated adequately will also help to prevent this form of meningitis.

## Other Forms of Meningitis

In rare cases, meningitis can be caused by chemical irritation (chemical meningitis) and tumors (carcinomatous meningitis). Although they are used infrequently, the chemicals responsible for chemical meningitis are often drugs, such as the ones administered to organ transplant recipients. But in extremely rare circumstances, over-the-counter painkillers have been known to cause the disease, too. Even some viruses like herpes simplex II can cause multiple occurrences of meningitis separated by periods of remission. This is called Mollaret's meningitis.

# 2

# BACTERIAL MENINGITIS

The bacteria that cause meningitis often live in a person's mouth, throat, or intestines, where they are not dangerous. Sometimes, however, these bacteria migrate to the spinal cord and brain, where they can seriously endanger a person's life.

The bacteria that cause meningitis are contagious, but close contact with an infected person is required in order to catch the disease. Casual contact with an infected person or something he or she touched will not normally spread this type of bacteria, although bacteria from meningococcal meningitis can be airborne. (For this reason, people exhibiting meningococcal meningitis symptoms are commonly isolated while undergoing treatment.) In most cases, health-care personnel do not consider a person with meningitis to be a serious danger to the community. However, there is a chance that he or she can spread the disease to others with whom he or she has close contact.

When someone is diagnosed with bacterial meningitis, the members of his or her family are usually treated with antibiotics. Although doctors do not know if they have been exposed to the disease, no one can predict if they will develop a case of meningitis or not. One of the main antibiotics used to treat family members, or anyone else who has been exposed to bacterial meningitis, is called Rifampin.

Three types of bacteria commonly cause meningitis. *Neisseria meningitidis* causes meningococcal meningitis. In some cases, meningococcal meningitis can cause death within only a few hours of the onset of symptoms. A vaccine has been developed against four of the thirteen groups of *N. meningitidis* (A, C, Y, and W-135, while the B, D, H, I, K, L, X, Z, and 29-E groups are still without vaccines), but they are usually ineffective for very young children.

It is estimated that at least 10 percent of the population carries *N. meningitidis* in their nasal and throat passages. In closed communities like military barracks, for example, the bacteria may be found in as much as 50 percent of the population. This particular meningitis is the form most closely associated with the development of a rash.

Carriers of *N. meningitidis* may have the bacteria in the nose and throat for days, weeks, or even months. However, it has not been possible to predict outbreaks of meningitis merely by finding populations where many people are carriers. Just because the bacteria are present does not mean people will begin to develop meningococcal meningitis in great numbers.

*Haemophilus influenzae* type b (Hib) was much more common before 1990. Since then, children have been vaccinated against *H. influenzae* type b. In 1987, the incidence of this disease in the population among children five years of age and younger was 421 cases per 100,000 in the United States. A decade later, the incidence had dropped significantly. This drop in the occurrence of meningitis in children has meant that the average age at

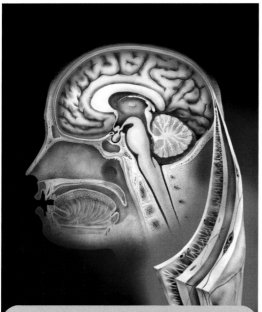

*This illustration shows a cross-section of a meninges (at right) affected by bacterial meningitis. The illustration shows how meningitis inflames the tissues and creates fluid that fills the spaces between the layers of the meninges.*

which people develop this form of meningitis has risen from fifteen months to twenty-five years.

*Streptococcus pneumoniae*, the most common form of bacterial meningitis, causes pneumococcal meningitis. A vaccine against the bacteria has been developed, but it is ineffective in children under two years of age. However, the vaccine is recommended for all persons over sixty-five. Although there are treatment options available today, many people still die from this form of meningitis. Survival rates for pneumococcal meningitis are 56 to 81 percent. These rates may not improve much in the future, as drug-resistant strains of *S. pneumoniae* are becoming more common. *S. pneumoniae* is often found in healthy people, though those who succumb to the disease are the elderly.

## Other Forms of Bacterial Meningitis

Together, these three previous organisms account for nearly 80 percent of diagnosed cases of bacterial meningitis in the United States. Many of the remaining cases are caused by other bacteria such as *Streptococcus agalactiae* and *Listeria monocytogenes*.

*S. agalactiae* is a group B streptococcus that normally lives in the lower intestines and most often causes meningitis in newborns. The survival rate for those with this form of bacterial meningitis is 66 percent.

Meningitis from *L. monocytogenes* is becoming more common. Before 1981, it accounted for only 2 percent of bacterial meningitis cases, but by 1995, this rate had risen to 8 percent. It primarily affects people who are immunosuppressed (individuals suffering from another disease, like cancer or AIDS, and transplant patients who already have a compromised immune system), infants, and the elderly. Meningitis outbreaks of this type have been linked with the consumption of contaminated foods like raw meat, milk, and cheese.

Rarely, meningitis may also be caused by spirochetes, which are another form of bacteria. The two most common spirochetes that cause meningitis are *Treponema pallidum*, which causes syphilitic meningitis, and *Borrelia burgdorferi*, which causes Lyme meningitis.

*T. pallidum* is normally acquired through sexual contact, through the placenta, or from blood transfusions. If left untreated, the meningitis symptoms will last for months and can result in stroke or brain damage.

*B. burgdorferi* is acquired from a tick infected with the spirochete. Ticks in Europe, North America, and Asia carry this particular bacterium. One particular symptom of Lyme meningitis is uncontrollable weakness in the facial muscles due to damage to the nerves, a condition commonly called Bell's palsy. Patients with this symptom may experience muscle weakness in one side of the face that causes it to droop. This form of meningitis is not usually fatal, but if left untreated, its symptoms may last for months.

At the dawn of the twentieth century, the most widespread form of meningitis was tubercular meningitis, caused by the bacteria *Mycobacterium tuberculosis*. Today, this form of meningitis is extremely rare because most people with tuberculosis (TB) actively seek medical attention to treat the disease before it progresses to meningitis, or because the bacteria often enters a patient's lungs and not his or her meninges.

Strains of TB still threaten the population, however, especially those who are old or already ill with another disease. (In 2001, there were approximately 16,000 cases of TB in the United States alone.) By the time the classic meningitis symptoms of stiff neck and headache occur in cases of TB-related meningitis, scarring of the lungs, or even a stroke may have already happened. Some elderly patients never develop a headache at all. They might become confused and lapse into a coma before their meningitis is even diagnosed. For this reason, it is very important for doctors who treat the elderly to be aware of the symptoms of tuberculosis and to recognize the danger of it developing into meningitis.

# 3

# HISTORY OF THE DISEASE

The classic symptoms of meningitis have been recognized as fatal for thousands of years. An ancient Mesopotamian incantation mentions a headache that roams through the desert, striking down men with scorching pain and confusion and inevitably resulting in death. Although we can't know for sure, it appears the author of the incantation was familiar with the symptoms of meningitis and recognized the terrible toll it took on its victims. Because of the lack of medical knowledge at the time, the author assumes the disease has a divine connection and claims it attacks those who have no god to protect them.

The first steps in learning about meningitis required understanding the anatomy of the brain and spinal cord. The ancient Greeks were the first to look inside the body and describe the various structures they saw. Hippocrates (460–377 BC), known as the Father of Medicine, was the first to guess at a connection between headache and an inflammation of the linings surrounding the brain. He also noted that when a stiff neck accompanied a headache and fever, death was often the result.

In the second century AD, the Greek physician Galen was the first to record an account of the clear fluid that could be found in the linings of the living brain. Galen did not understand what the fluid was, and he and future physicians considered it abnormal.

In 1825, François Magendie (1783–1855) circulated an obscure

*François Magendie* (above) *proved an important theory on the motor function of spinal nerves. He also introduced the use of morphine and other drugs into medicine.*

work by Domenico Cotugno, who had written in 1764 that the spinal fluid and cerebral fluid were the same substance. As scientists and physicians already understood that spinal fluid was a normal part of the body, the fact that the fluid surrounding the spine and brain were the same was one more step toward understanding the nervous system.

# Identifying Meningitis

Because the anatomy of the meninges and the presence of cerebrospinal fluid remained mysterious, meningitis was not clearly recognized as a disease for many centuries. In fact, no clear description of a meningitis outbreak exists before the nineteenth century.

In 1805, a Swiss physician named Gaspard Vieusseux gave an eyewitness account of a meningitis outbreak in the town of Eaux-Vives on Lake Geneva in Switzerland. Thirty-three people died. The disease was described as "malignant purpuric fever," and the symptoms were listed as a terrible headache, vomiting, stiffness in the neck and spine, and rashes on the skin. A local pathologist who conducted an autopsy on one of the victims found pus at the base of his brain.

Nine cases, all of them fatal, were recorded a year later in 1806 in Massachusetts. The symptoms were of a classic meningitis outbreak: sudden terrible headaches, nausea, chills, rashes, and confusion, followed by seizures, coma, and death. The instances were reported in a letter to the editor of the *Medical and Agricultural Register*.

In 1811, Elisha North of Connecticut published a collection of such cases and correctly noted that rashes were not evident in each person. North felt that the name "spotted fever," which some gave to the disease, was inaccurate.

Other meningitis outbreaks of the nineteenth century appeared in North America, Europe, and the Fiji Islands. These cases attracted interest from a variety of physicians and scientists, but they did not yet have the tools necessary to properly diagnose or treat the disease.

# Oscar Wilde

Oscar Wilde (1854–1900) was an Irish author famous for his plays, poetry, and fiction. His first publication, a collection of poems, was distributed in 1881. That same year, he traveled to the United States for an extended lecturing tour. One of his most famous pieces is the novel *The Picture of Dorian Gray*, which is a story about a man whose portrait ages while he remains young. He also wrote several plays that are still staged  in many theaters around the world. They include *The Importance of Being Earnest* and *An Ideal Husband*. Recently, Hollywood turned these plays into movies. *An Ideal Husband* was released in 1999, and *The Importance of Being Earnest* was released in 2002.

Like many other authors, Wilde's personal life was tragic and marred by scandal. The last several years of his life were spent in exile in Italy and France. By the time of his death in 1900, he was penniless and living alone in a hotel in Paris.

*Oscar Wilde* (above) *was imprisoned for his writings in 1895. The harsh conditions of prison life might also have weakened his immune system and made it easier for him to contract meningitis.*

Wilde's health declined in 1899 with what he referred to as "mussel poisoning." Wilde broke out in an itchy rash and claimed that his throat burned and his brain was on fire. For four months, he stayed in bed most of the time, rising only for a short while in the afternoons. He complained he did not even have the energy to write letters. Some researchers today diagnose his malady as syphilis.

By September 1900, Wilde was bedridden. A doctor named Maurice Tucker attended Wilde during his illness and, knowing he had recurrent ear infections, advised an operation. A surgeon operated on Wilde in his hotel room on October 10. However, Wilde's plight was not improved.

On October 29, Wilde left his bed for the first time in weeks. He and a friend went to a café where Wilde drank a large quantity of alcohol. His friend feared this would not be good for Wilde's health, and indeed, the next day, Wilde complained of a terrible pain in his ear. The doctor suggested a ride in the country, but Wilde insisted on stopping at every café for more alcohol and was soon feeling very ill. The ride was cut short, and Wilde returned to his hotel room.

By November 6, even morphine was not helping Wilde's pain. His condition deteriorated until by November 26, he was periodically delusional. On the 29th, his confusion lifted a little, though he was still in agony. He died November 30.

The bacteria that killed Wilde may have migrated to his brain from the operation site in his ear. Or it may have been due to Wilde's lengthy illness that may or may not have been syphilis. In either case, the bacteria escaped to his brain. From that point on, there was no treatment available and death was certain. Debate continues to rage to this day over which form of meningitis killed Oscar Wilde.

# Understanding the Role of Bacteria

Real progress toward solving the mystery of meningitis was not made until after 1876. That was the year Robert Koch identified the organism that causes anthrax. After he correctly associated a particular organism with a disease, scientists began to study bacteria more carefully. This quickly led to the first discovery of a foreign bacterium in the cerebrospinal fluid of a meningitis patient in 1887 by Anton Weichselbaum. In fact, within approximately eleven years of Koch's anthrax discovery, all of the major bacterial causes of meningitis had been identified.

But identifying the bacteria during an autopsy was only the first step. The next step was in discovering how to diagnose meningitis in a living patient. In 1891, Heinrich Quincke developed a technique for taking cerebrospinal fluid from a patient through a lumbar puncture. Other physicians, such as Ludwig Lichtheim, observed the changes in cerebrospinal fluid that occurred during a meningitis infection. In 1893, Lichtheim published his discovery that the cerebrospinal fluid of meningitis patients had low glucose concentrations. For the next century, analysis of glucose in cerebrospinal fluid was one of the major tools used to diagnose the disease.

During the twentieth century, further diagnostic tests were discovered and utilized. However, simply diagnosing meningitis was not enough. Scientists wanted to find ways to effectively treat and cure the disease. The pressure to find a way to treat meningitis became more intense as more deadly epidemics swept through cities, killing about 70 percent of those infected.

## Addie Joss

Adrian C. "Addie" Joss (1880–1911) was a pitcher for the Cleveland Bluebirds (later the Cleveland Indians) from 1902 to 1910. Joss had a career earned run average (ERA) of 1.88, which is the second best of all time. He pitched two no-hitters during his career and finished 234 of his 260 starts. Joss won twenty or more games each year from 1905 to 1908. During the 1909 season, however, he fought arm injuries and took the mound in only thirteen games.

On April 3, 1911, Joss walked out onto a field in Chattanooga, Tennessee, and collapsed. He was rushed to a hospital, where doctors diagnosed heat prostration due to the intense heat and humidity of the day. Joss was released that evening.

Joss caught a train to catch up with his teammates, who were on their way to Cincinnati. However, he began having chest pains and changed his destination to Toledo to see his personal doctor, Dr. George W. Chapman. Chapman made note of Joss's pains, his lack of appetite, and sudden weight loss, and diagnosed nervous indigestion. He thought it might possibly have been caused by food poisoning. (Since baseball players were often on the road, food poisoning was a likely consequence of their hectic schedules.)

*Addie Joss, seen here on a circa 1909 American Tobacco Company collectible card, was admitted into the Baseball Hall of Fame in 1978, sixty-seven years after his death from meningitis. Joss was known for his "pinwheel" pitch.*

Joss, assured that he would recover, walked to the local newspaper office to visit his friends on the staff. They were not prepared for the sight of a thinning, sunken Joss. Even the pitcher's speech was slurred. It appeared to the reporters that Joss was terribly ill, but Joss told them he would be all right in time.

Joss began coughing constantly. On April 9, Dr. Chapman saw Joss again and revised his diagnosis to pleurisy, an infection in the membranes surrounding the lungs. The doctor reported to the team that Joss would not be able to play baseball for at least a month. Dr. Chapman advised Joss to stay at home for ten days.

Joss did not get better. Soon he had developed a severe headache. Dr. Chapman realized this was not a symptom of pleurisy. Joss was ill with something else, but Dr. Chapman was unsure what it might be. He called the baseball team's doctor and asked him to examine Joss immediately. The doctor caught a train and arrived at the Joss home on the morning of April 13. He performed a lumbar puncture, examined the cerebrospinal fluid, and soon realized that Joss had meningitis. The weight loss, lack of appetite, and coughing pointed to tubercular meningitis, the most common form of the disease at the time. And then, at some point, the bacteria that caused the tuberculosis migrated to Joss's brain.

In 1911, there was no treatment for meningitis. All the doctors could do was administer painkillers to try to keep the severe headache under control. On Friday, April 14, 1911, Addie Joss died.

## Treatment

When epidemics of meningococcal meningitis hit New York in 1904 and 1905, more than 5,000 people died. Germany was also struck with meningitis epidemics in

**1805**
First description of a meningitis outbreak that took place in Switzerland.

**1887**
*N. meningitidis* is identified as one cause of meningitis.

**1891**
Procedure for extracting cerebrospinal fluid through a lumbar puncture is first performed.

**1900**
Oscar Wilde, author, dies of meningitis.

**1904–1905**
New York experiences an epidemic that kills approximately 5,000 people.

**1911**
Addie Joss, baseball pitcher, dies of tubercular meningitis.

**1914–1918**
World War I, meningitis anti-serum saves many lives.

the first decade of the twentieth century. Researchers in both countries worked hard to find solutions.

Within a few years, they had their first break-through. By injecting horses with heat-killed bacteria, the horses' immune systems produced anti-bodies against the bacteria. The researchers then

**1930s**
Sulfonamides first used to combat meningitis.

**1940s**
Penicillin first used to combat meningitis.

**1966**
Vaccines first developed for some forms of meningitis.

**1990s**
Vaccine for *H. influenzae* type b is given widely to children in the United States; rates of meningitis due to this bacteria plunge.

**1996**
More than 20,000 people die in the meningitis belt.

**2003**
The World Health Organization (WHO) requests money from charitable organizations to purchase six million doses of the meningitis vaccine for people living in the meningitis belt.

**2004**
Missouri becomes the twenty-eighth state to require a meningitis vaccine for college students living in public housing.

created an antiserum from the horses' blood and injected this into people suffering from meningitis. In one of the first trials, the mortality rate among those treated dropped from 70 to 30 percent.

At first, antiserum was injected into the bloodstream, but further tests showed that injecting it directly into the spine was much more effective. However, the use of the antiserum led to a new disease that scientists called "serum sickness." Up to 50 percent of patients treated with the antiserum developed fevers, skin eruptions, arthritis, and digestive disorders.

Still, the antiserum was the only working treatment available at the time, and though it carried the risk of terrible side effects, it continued to be used and saved many lives. During World War I, the survival rate among military personnel with meningitis was 67 percent.

Antiserum was the mainstay of meningitis treatment into the 1930s. By then, the United States had experienced even more meningitis epidemics, including those that occurred in Detroit, Milwaukee, and Indianapolis during 1928 and 1929. Because many of the infected were infants unable to fight off the disease or ingest the antiserum, the overall mortality rate jumped from 30 to 50 percent. The treatment had helped, but better solutions were desperately needed.

## Sulfa Drugs

In the mid-1930s, a different kind of treatment became available. Sulfonamides ("sulfa drugs") had first been developed in 1908, but their antibacterial properties weren't discovered for some time. In 1935, the first meningitis patient treated with a sulfonamide in the United States was a ten-year-old girl who had been stricken with *H. influenzae*.

In 1937, the *Journal of the American Medical Association* printed a report on the effectiveness of sulfonamides against meningococcal meningitis. The mortality rate for treatment with sulfonamides among the patients in the trial was 9 percent. The surviving patients did not experience side effects like earlier people had from the antiserum and tolerated the drugs well. Within a year, others had reproduced similar results in their own trials. Sulfonamides had become the treatment of choice for meningococcal meningitis by 1941. The use of antiserum for this form of the disease was discontinued.

Sulfonamides had become one of the first wonder drugs. However, though effective in combating meningococcal meningitis, they did little to help patients with other types of the disease. Pneumococcal meningitis, for instance, remained fatal in almost all cases.

During the 1940s, penicillin was introduced and became more effective at treating meningococcal meningitis than earlier treatments, nearly stopping this form of the disease in its tracks. However, no matter how effective the new drugs were against this type of meningitis, the other bacterial forms of the disease remained more difficult to treat.

# 4

# WHO IS AT RISK?

**A**nyone can develop a case of meningitis, but some people are more likely than others to become ill from the disease. Most of the bacteria that cause meningitis are not dangerous if they remain outside the cerebrospinal fluid. Usually, something has to happen to prompt them to migrate to the meninges from other areas of the body.

Strangely, one of the main places to get meningitis is in the hospital. This is because so many sick people are in a hospital that many dangerous organisms live there in enough quantity to make someone ill. The people who work in hospitals know that it is important to keep infections controlled so that sick people will not get infected with another illness. Still, even with precautions, 5.6 of every 100,000 discharged patients will have caught a central nervous system (CNS) infection in the hospital. More than 90 percent of these hospital-caught CNS infections will be meningitis. Unlike meningitis contracted outside the hospital, meningitis contracted inside the hospital is usually due to organisms like staphylococci, commonly known as staph infections.

Meningitis is also one of the complications that may arise after a head injury. The linings surrounding the brain are already damaged or even ruptured. It does not take much for bacteria to invade in that situation. Even minor head trauma, like a concussion, can increase the

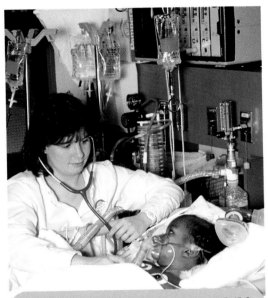

*A pediatric nurse attends a child suffering from severe meningitis. Young children are especially susceptible to the disease, though it can strike at any age.*

chances of developing meningitis. If the meninges are ruptured enough for cerebrospinal fluid to leak out, the chances are even greater. In such cases, the leak must be repaired or the person may suffer repeated attacks of bacterial meningitis. Cerebrospinal fluid leaks can be the result of motor vehicle accidents, accidental falls, or gunshot wounds, among other things. Patients who develop meningitis after head trauma develop pneumococcal meningitis. Infections from staphylococci are possible, but rare.

Surgeries to the head or spine may also result in meningitis. One of the main organisms that can cause meningitis in these cases is *Staphylococcus epidermidis*. This is usually found on the skin and is therefore most likely to have been introduced during surgery by the surgeons or from the patient's own skin.

However, one of the main risk factors for meningitis is age. As indicated earlier, meningitis is more common in infants and the elderly, although the incidence of meningitis in infants has now come down since the development of the vaccine for *H. influenzae*. Infants may still contract other forms of the disease, however, including meningococcal and pneumococcal meningitis. For children under two years of age, one of the main causes of meningitis is *Escherichia coli*, a common bacteria that normally lives in the intestines. However, in the past few years, group B streptococcus has become the most common cause of meningitis for those under one month of age, surpassing *E. coli*.

Factors determining whether an infant will develop meningitis include a low birth weight and meninges

In June 2001, citizens of Alliance, Ohio, lined up for preventative antibiotics at a local hospital after a meningitis outbreak. Two high school students died in the outbreak.

that have been ruptured due to a difficult birth or other trauma. Because staphylococcus can also be responsible for meningitis in infants, it is possible that many contract the disease from the hands of hospital personnel, according to *Infections of the Central Nervous System*, a book by W. Michael Scheld, Richard J. Whitley, and David T. Durack. In fact, premature or low-birth-weight infants are often at higher risk for an infection due to their immature immune systems.

# 5

# THE MENINGITIS BELT

The region of the world where meningitis is the most widespread and deadly is an area of sub-Saharan Africa often called the meningitis belt. This area extends from Mali in the west to Ethiopia in the east. This semi-arid region is also known as the Sahel. Meningitis is so common in the Sahel that what is a normal rate of infection there would be an epidemic anywhere else. The countries that report the most cases of meningitis are Burkina Faso, Mali, Niger, and Nigeria.

Doctors who have studied meningitis in Africa have recently realized that the disease is most widespread in areas where there are extreme differences between the seasons. In places where it is dry all year or humid all year, meningitis is present, but rare. However, in places with distinct dry and wet seasons, meningitis is more common. Epidemics occur regularly, often coming in eight- to twelve-year cycles. In these locations, the danger of meningitis increases during the dry months and disappears with the annual beginning of the rainy season.

One of the most common causes of meningitis in the meningitis belt is *N. meningitidis*, group A. During an epidemic, as much as 1 percent of the population of the area may be infected. Some researchers believe that the bacteria of group A often mutate so that the population is not able to acquire immunity to the bacteria. Normally, once many people have had a disease and survived, the entire population has what is called herd

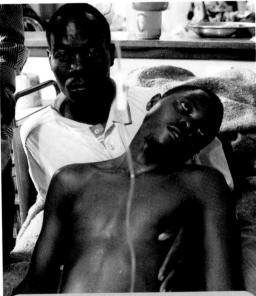

*An HIV-positive young man, critically ill with meningitis, is held by a relative in Lilongwe, Malawi, in 1998. The AIDS epidemic has worsened the incidence of meningitis and other diseases in many African countries.*

immunity. That means that enough people have had the disease that it can't spread very far. A few people might be affected, but too many are immune for the disease to become an epidemic.

Although group A *N. meningitidis* is common in the meningitis belt, W-135, is also on the rise. Until 1997, W-135 had not been known to be responsible for any meningitis cases, but by 2000, it accounted for 19 percent of the infections that were studied by researchers in the country of Cameroon.

One way in which new strains of meningitis are introduced to the meningitis belt is through the hajj. The hajj is a pilgrimage that most Muslims make to Mecca in Saudi Arabia at least once in their lives. Much of the population of the meningitis belt is Muslim, and therefore, many of them travel to Saudi Arabia.

Because of this, Saudi Arabia requires that all hajj pilgrims be vaccinated against meningitis. The quadrivalent vaccine for pilgrims protects against groups A, C, Y, and W-135. In the spring of 2000, pilgrims and those with whom they had close contact experienced an epidemic of W-135. By the time it was over, 241 cases had been reported in Saudi Arabia and 90 in other countries, including the United States, France, and Great Britain.

Vaccines for some of the groups of *N. meningitidis* are available, but there are not necessarily large numbers of doses available to poor countries like those in the meningitis belt. In September 2003, the World Health Organization (WHO) issued a statement that time was running out in its effort to raise money to buy vaccines

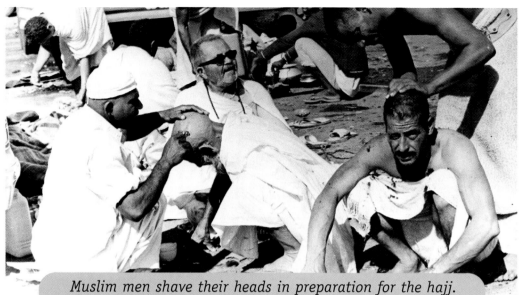

*Muslim men shave their heads in preparation for the hajj. According to the British Broadcasting Corporation (BBC), the number of cases of meningitis contracted during the hajj had fallen from thirty-eight cases in 2002 to six cases in 2003, due to increased inoculations. No deaths from meningitis were reported after the 2003 hajj.*

before the beginning of the 2004 meningitis season. Although the independent international medical relief organization Doctors Without Borders (Medecins sans Frontieres) said it would purchase one million doses, that was only one-sixth of the total doses the WHO estimated it would need. The other five million doses would have to be funded by governments and charitable donations.

In the future, such economic and political realities behind meningitis epidemics may leave many people vulnerable. Even if help is available, it may not reach those who need it most.

# 6

# SURVIVING MENINGITIS

**M**any people in the United States who have meningitis survive. However, they must deal with the consequences of the infection. Some of these consequences are minor and some are not. It is important for meningitis survivors to know how their lives might be affected right away, and in the long-term.

Fortunately, most people do not suffer serious consequences from the disease. They leave the hospital feeling much better and look forward to an easy recovery. Some are not so lucky.

Being in the hospital is a very upsetting experience. Children who have been hospitalized for meningitis often experience changes in behavior after they come home. They are likely to have nightmares and be extra clingy with their parents, and may demand more attention. If the child was a bed wetter at some point in the past, he or she may revert to that behavior. Some children will begin to throw tantrums, even if they didn't do so before the infection. Often, they will have to relearn skills they acquired shortly before becoming sick. Rarely, they will begin to sleepwalk. Another possible conse-quence of a menin-gitis infection is for a child to frequently become sick with minor illnesses, like colds, for a while.

Because most of these effects may be due to the stress of the hospi-talization rather than the meningitis itself, patience and understand-ing are the best remedies for the behaviors.

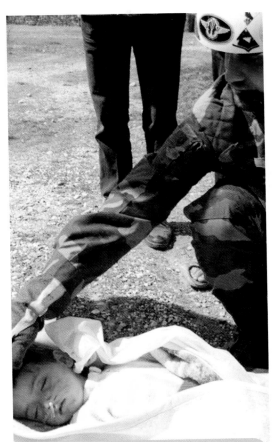

*A helicopter pilot cares for a young refugee ill with meningitis during the Kosovo crisis. The incidence of diseases such as meningitis often increases in wartime.*

Some people experience physical changes due to the meningitis infection. These complications recede within several weeks or months. They include:

- ⊛ Being tired
- ⊛ Recurrent headaches
- ⊛ Clumsiness
- ⊛ Mood swings
- ⊛ Problems with balance
- ⊛ Difficulty concentrating

The more severe complications of a meningitis infection can include:

- ⊛ Deafness
- ⊛ Ringing in the ears
- ⊛ Difficulty seeing
- ⊛ Seizures
- ⊛ Aggressive behavior
- ⊛ Stiffness in the joints
- ⊛ Brain damage
- ⊛ The need for skin grafts
- ⊛ Amputation

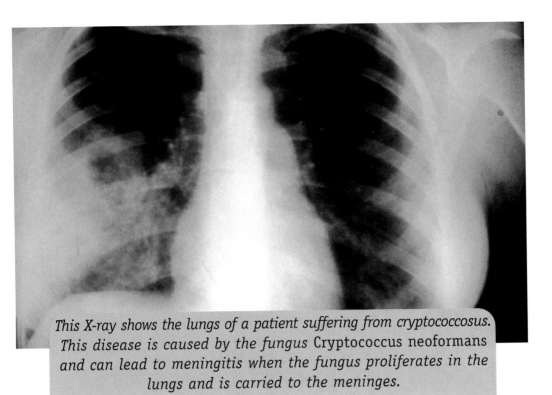

*This X-ray shows the lungs of a patient suffering from cryptococcosus. This disease is caused by the fungus Cryptococcus neoformans and can lead to meningitis when the fungus proliferates in the lungs and is carried to the meninges.*

One of the most common of these serious complications is deafness. This affects about 10 percent of the people who have meningitis. This deafness may only be short term, or it may be lifelong. It is important for anyone who has had meningitis to have a hearing test after he or she gets well. Small children should be tested because they may not be able to tell anyone about their hearing loss.

If the infection affects not only the meninges, but also enters the bloodstream, the person can develop blood poisoning. This is called septicemia. It can result in the need to amputate fingers or toes, or even entire limbs. Or it can cause such severe damage and scarring that skin grafts will have to be performed to help an area heal.

The fortunate thing is that these more serious complications are somewhat rare. More commonly, a person recovering from meningitis will experience general fatigue. Because "being tired" is something others can't see, other people might not understand how poor the recovering person is feeling. It is important for people recovering from meningitis to be careful with their activity level and rest when they feel they need to.

Many people feel they should rush back into the same schedule they had before they got sick. They don't realize it may take months for them to recover fully. If a person has unrealistic expectations, he or she may feel depressed upon realizing how long it will take to feel completely well. In time, though, most people who have survived meningitis will resume their old schedules.

# 7

# THE FUTURE OF MENINGITIS

Meningitis has been deadly for thousands of years. But it was not until the twentieth century that doctors could reliably diagnose and treat the disease. For that reason, meningitis is less dangerous now than it was in the past. Still, because it can be caused by viruses, bacteria, fungi, parasites, or in rare cases, chemicals, we will always need to research new ways to treat the disease. And we will need to be on the lookout for cases of meningitis from new diseases. As viruses make their way around the world to populations that have never experienced them before, new forms of meningitis will likely be seen along with them. Today, scientists are very concerned about a virus that has made its way to the United States quite recently: West Nile virus.

# West Nile and Meningitis

West Nile virus had first been described in the African country of Uganda in 1937. After that, it spread to Egypt and Israel, and in the 1960s, France. By the 1990s, West Nile had spread farther than ever before. It was first seen in Algeria in 1994, Romania in 1996, the Czech Republic in 1997, and Russia in 1999. Scientists who predicted it would reach the United States were correct in their assumptions. West Nile was discovered in birds in the northeastern United States in 1999.

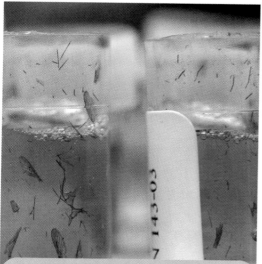

*These mosquitoes were captured to be tested for West Nile virus in 2003, in California. West Nile has been on the rise in the United States since 1999.*

The virus quickly spread to humans (who had been bitten by infected mosquitoes) and went far beyond the northeastern section of the country all the way to the West Coast. In 2002, 4,156 human cases were reported to the Centers for Disease Control and Prevention (CDC). In 2003, 9,858 cases were reported. Of these, 262 were fatal. In the future, West Nile is likely to infect even greater numbers of people and cause even more deaths.

Researchers were not waiting to see what would happen as West Nile spread. They were actively trying to figure out how to treat people and how to educate the population to avoid infection, and especially, to know what the possible consequences of the virus would be in the future.

One consequence that worried researchers was that West Nile, like so many other viruses, might possibly cause meningitis. Meningitis can be caused by other viruses spread by mosquitoes, such as St. Louis encephalitis and LaCrosse encephalitis, so this was not a casual fear. Viral meningitis may rarely be fatal, but it is still a serious disease, and the researchers could not afford to not look for a connection.

## Outbreak

In the summer of 2001, researchers noted that a viral meningitis outbreak in Baltimore coincided with the occurrence of West Nile virus. (One hundred thirteen cases of viral meningitis were identified.) The researchers decided to search for a connection between the two diseases.

To determine if a connection existed, researchers identified the viruses responsible in as many cases as

*A Colorado Mosquito Control helicopter sprays insecticide to counteract West Nile virus near Fort Collins, Colorado, in 2003. The virus had already killed thirteen elderly people in Colorado when this photo was taken.*

possible. However, 61 percent of patients who were tested caught meningitis from enteroviruses. The two main culprits behind the epidemic were the echoviruses 13 and 18. No cases of meningitis caused by West Nile could be found.

For Baltimore in 2001, West Nile was not a cause of meningitis. However, in the future, it may cause meningitis in other cities. Researchers will have to remain alert, not only for West Nile, but for any other new viruses, since any of them could become a source of meningitis outbreak.

For sixty years, penicillin was the main weapon against bacterial meningitis, but today several strains of bacteria (especially *S. pneumoniae*) have evolved that are resistant to penicillin. Doctors have turned to other antibiotics for help, but even these are losing their effectiveness. New drugs can be effective, but in the end, bacteria will win out if nothing is done to eradicate them from populations.

## Prevention by Vaccination

The best way to get rid of some forms of meningitis is through vaccination. Today's vaccines can protect people from some of the more common forms of the disease, but not from all of them. The success of severely reducing the number of *H. influenza*e type b infections in the United States during the 1990s shows that widespread vaccination works. However, there still is no vaccine for one of the main causes of bacterial meningitis, *N. meningitidis* (group B).

In countries where meningitis is a greater danger than in the United States, like those in the meningitis belt, the main problem is economic. The vaccines that are available must be provided by organizations like the WHO, Doctors Without Borders, or other charities or government groups. In the future, many people will continue to go without the option of vaccinations because they live in poor countries that cannot afford the number of doses required.

Currently, we cannot see a time when we can wipe out meningitis entirely. Meningitis is caused by too many

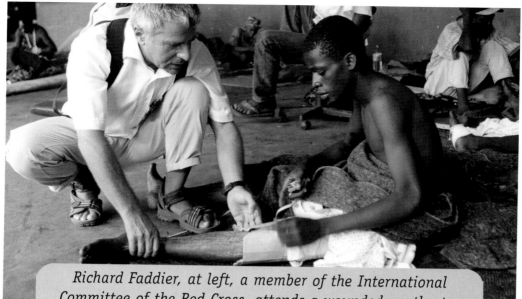

Richard Faddier, at left, a member of the International Committee of the Red Cross, attends a wounded youth at a hospital in Monrovia, Liberia. Groups such as the Red Cross and Doctors Without Borders are on the front lines in treating wounds and preventing disease in war-torn countries without a reliable health-care system.

different things—viruses, bacteria, fungi, and parasites. Vaccines will help reduce the incidence of viral and bacterial forms, but improvement in living conditions will be needed to reduce the number of parasitic infections. Fungal infections will continue to occur as long as people have diseases that attack their immune systems. A weak immune system will leave people vulnerable to the fungi found in everyday environments.

Researchers and doctors have made great headway in their diagnosis and treatment of the disease, antibiotics have saved many lives, and a few vaccines are available. But as far as we can see now, meningitis will be with us for a long time to come.

# GLOSSARY

**antiserum** A treatment for meningitis developed by injecting horses with heat-killed bacteria and then developing a serum from the horses' blood.

***Borrelia burgdorferi*** A spirochete bacterium that causes Lyme meningitis.

**cerebrospinal fluid** The fluid that surrounds and protects the brain and spinal chord.

***Coccidioides immitis*** A fungus that causes meningitis.

**coxsackie** A kind of enterovirus that causes meningitis.

**echovirus** A kind of enterovirus that causes meningitis.

**enterovirus** A kind of virus that normally lives in the intestines.

*Escherichia coli*  A specific bacterium that normally lives in the intestines and is a common cause of meningitis in infants.

*Haemophilus influenzae* (type b)  One of the three most common bacteria to cause meningitis in the United States.

immune system  The body's main defense against disease.

*Listeria monocytogenes*  A bacterium that causes meningitis.

meninges  The three layers of membranes around the brain: the innermost layer is known as the pia mater, followed by the central arachnoid layer, and the outer dura mater.

meningitis  An infection of the cerebrospinal fluid around the brain and the meninges.

meningitis, bacterial  Meningitis caused by a bacterium.

meningitis belt  An area of Africa where meningitis rates are the highest in the world.

meningitis, carcinomatous  Meningitis caused by cancerous tumors.

meningitis, coccidioidal  Meningitis caused by the fungus *C. immitis*.

meningitis, fungal  Meningitis caused by a fungus.

meningitis, Lyme  A form of meningitis caused by a tick-borne bacterium, *B. burgdorferi*.

**meningitis, meningococcal** Meningitis caused by
*N. meningitidis.*

**meningitis, Mollaret's** A recurrent form of meningitis
caused by various viruses, often herpes simplex II.

**meningitis, parasitic** Meningitis caused by
roundworm or amoebic infection.

**meningitis, pneumococcal** Meningitis caused by
*S. pneumoniae.*

**meningitis, syphilitic** A form of meningitis caused
by the bacterium that causes syphilis, *T. pallidum.*

**meningitis, tubercular** Meningitis caused by *M.
tuberculosis.*

**meningitis, viral** Meningitis caused by a virus.

*Mycobacterium tuberculosis* The bacterium that
causes tubercular meningitis.

*Naegleria fowleri* A kind of amoeba that causes
meningitis.

*Neisseria meningitidis* One of the three most
common bacteria to cause meningitis in the
United States.

**penicillin** An antibiotic developed from mold and
first used against meningitis in the 1940s.

**primary amebic meningoencephalitis** The
kind of meningitis caused by the amoeba
*N. fowleri.*

**rat lungworm** A worm that can cause parasitic
meningitis.

**serum sickness**  A reaction to the injection of antiserum; can include fevers, joint disorders, and skin problems.

**spirochete**  A bacterium that is in a spiral form.

*Staphylococcus epidermidis*  A bacterium that is normally found on human skin and that may cause meningitis in certain patients who have had surgeries to the head or spine.

**streptococcus**  A strain of parasitic bacteria that infects humans and domestic animals.

*Streptococcus agalactiae*  A group B streptococcus that causes bacterial meningitis.

*Streptococcus pneumoniae*  One of the three most common bacteria to cause meningitis in the United States.

*Strongyloides stercoralis*  A kind of worm that can cause parasitic meningitis.

**sulfonamides**  Drugs developed from sulfanilic acid that were the first drugs to be used against meningitis; also known as sulfa drugs.

**syphilis**  A sexually transmitted disease.

*Treponema pallidum*  A spirochete bacterium that causes syphilitic meningitis.

**vaccine**  An injection of a substance that is given to make the body produce defense mechanisms against a certain disease.

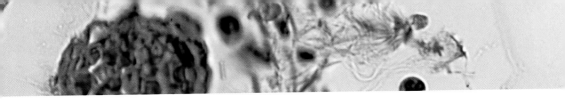

# FOR MORE INFORMATION

## In the United States

The Centers for Disease Control and
  Prevention (CDC)
1600 Clifton Road
Atlanta, GA 30333
(800) 311-3435
Web site: http://www.cdc.gov

The National Meningitis Association, Inc.
22910 Chestnut Road
Lexington Park, MD 20653
(866) 366-3662
Web site: http://www.nmaus.org

## In Canada

Canadian Coalition for Immunization Awareness
  and Promotion
Canadian Public Health Association
P500-1565 Carling Avenue
Ottawa, ON K1Z 8R1
(613) 725-3769
e-mail: immunize@cpha.ca
Web site: http://www.immunize.cpha.ca

Meningitis Research Foundation of Canada
P.O. Box 28015 R.P.O. Parkdale
Waterloo, ON N2L 6J8
(519) 746-8306
Web site: http://www.meningitis.ca

## Web Sites

Due to the changing nature of Internet links, the
Rosen Publishing Group, Inc., has developed an
online list of Web sites related to the subject of this
book. This site is updated regularly. Please use this
link to access the list:

http://www.rosenlinks.com/epid/meni

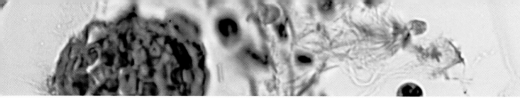

# FOR FURTHER READING

Brunelle, Lynn, and Marc Gave, editors. *Viruses* (Discovery Channel School Science). Milwaukee, WI: Gareth Stevens Publishing, 2003.

Ravage, Barbara, and Lynn Brunelle, editors. *Bacteria* (Discovery Channel School Science). Milwaukee, WI: Gareth Stevens Publishing, 2003.

Routh, Kristina. *Meningitis* (Just the Facts). Portsmouth, NH: Heinemann Library, 2004.

Snedden, Robert. *Fighting Infectious Diseases*. Barrington, IL: Heinemann Library, 2000.

# BIBLIOGRAPHY

Centers for Disease Control and Prevention. "Aseptic
    Meningitis Epidemic During a West Nile Virus Avian
    Epizootic." Retrieved January 16, 2004 (http://
    www. cdc.gov/ncidod/EID/vol9no9/03-0068.htm).
Centers for Disease Control and Prevention. "Aseptic
    Meningitis—New York State and United States,
    Weeks 1–36, 1991." Retrieved January 6, 2004
    (http://www. cdc.gov/mmwr/preview/mmwrhtml/
    00015566.htm).
Centers for Disease Control and Prevention.
    "Meningococcal Disease." Retrieved November 13,
    2003 (http://www.cdc. gov/ncidod/dbmd/
    diseaseinfo/meningococcal_g.htm).
Centers for Disease Control and Prevention. "Statistics,
    Surveillance, and Control: West Nile Virus 2003
    Case Count." Retrieved January 22, 2004 (http://

www.cdc.gov/ ncidod/dvbid/westnile/ surv&controlCaseCount03. htm).

Committee on Infectious Diseases, American Academy of Pediatrics. *Report of the Committee on Infectious Diseases*, twenty-second edition. Elk Grove Village, IL: American Academy of Pediatrics, 1991.

Medical-Conditions.org. "Meningitis." Retrieved January 26, 2004 (http://www.medical-conditions .org/?q=Meningitis).

Meningitis Foundation of America. "Viral Meningitis." Retrieved January 5, 2004 (http://www.musa.org/ fact4.htm).

Neurologychannel. "Meningitis Overview." Retrieved January 26, 2004 (http://www.neurologychannel .com/meningitis).

Parker, James N., M.D., and Philip M. Parker, Ph.D., editors. *The Official Patient's Sourcebook on Meningitis: A Revised and Updated Directory for the Internet Age*. San Diego: ICON Health Publications, 2002.

Tunkel, Allan R. *Bacterial Meningitis*. Philadelphia: Lippincott Williams & Wilkins, 2001.

Warnock, David, M.D. "Fungal Meningitis." Meningitis Foundation of America. Retrieved January 6, 2004 (http://www.musa.org/ fungal.htm).

World Health Organization. "Meningitis." Retrieved January 26, 2004 (http://www.who.int/health_ topics/meningitis/en).

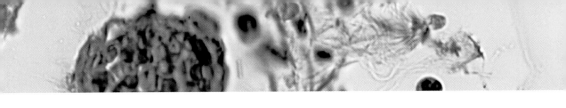

# INDEX

# CREDITS

## About the Author

Martha Kneib is a native St. Louisian who holds a master's degree in anthropology. She devotes most of her time to writing, maintaining her Web site, and traveling with her husband. This is her sixth book for the Rosen Publishing Group.

## Photo Credits